BEGINNINGS

ANIMALS

ORIGINS AND EVOLUTION

EVOLUTION OF THE UNIVERSE

4.5 billion years ago the oceans and first landmasses form.

9

1 million years after the Big Bang, hydrogen atoms form.

5

10-20 billion years ago, in less than a second, four things happen.

1. The Big Bang
2. Inflation
3. The beginning of the four forces
4. The first atomic nuclei form

1 billion years after the Big Bang, galaxies begin to form.

6

8 4.6 billion years ago the Earth's crust forms.

7 5 billion years ago the planet Earth forms.

11 2.5 billion years ago the atmosphere forms.

10 3 billion years ago bacteria appear— life begins.

BEGINNINGS

Animals

ORIGINS AND EVOLUTION

by
Cristiano Dal Sasso

English Translation by Rocco Serini

Belitha Press

First published in the United Kingdom in 1994 by

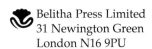 Belitha Press Limited
31 Newington Green
London N16 9PU

English translation © 1994 by Steck-Vaughn Company.

Cataloguing in print data available from the British Library.

ISBN 1 85561 378 6

Photographs GIANNI ARCUDI, Milan p. 4 (1,4). ALLESSANDRO BOESI, Milan: p. 4 (8). DAVIDE DE CERIOLI, Nicorvo, Pavia: p. 4 (2). CRISTIANO DAL SASSO, Milan: p. 25 (3), p. 28 (1), p. 29 (2), p. 34 (5, 6, 7), p. 15 (3, 4), p. 18 (1), p. 19 (4, 5), p. 21 (3, 4, 5), p. 25 (5), p. 26 (2), p. 27 (4, 5), p. 28 (4), p. 33 (3, 4, 5, 6), p. 34 (1), p. 35 (2, 3, 4, 10), p. 36 (2). GIOVANNI PINNA, Milan: p. 4 (6), p. 17 (4). p. 25 (2, 4), p. 26 (1), p. 27 (3), p. 29 (5), p. 30 (1). GORGIO TERUZZI, Milan: p. 4 (3, 7), p. 14 (1), p. 16 (2), p. 19 (2, 3), p. 32 (2).

Illustrations Editoriale Jaca Book, Milan (Severino Baraldi): p. 37 (3); (Remo Berselli): p. 4 (5), p. 6-7, p. 12-13, p. 20 (1), p. 22-23, p. 36 (1); (Cesare Dattena): p. 5 (9), p. 16 (1, 2, 3), p. 24 (1), p. 26 (7, 8), p. 27 (9), p. 29 (6, 7, 8), p. 30 (2), p. 35 (11); (Rosalba Morrigia e Maria Piatto): p. 8, p. 19 (6); (Lorenzo Orlandi): p. 8 (1), p. 9 (2), p. 15 (2), p. 17 (5), p. 29 (3), p. 32 (1); (Mario Tamer): p. 31 (3).
Illustration p. 10 (2) is from *Early Life*, published by Science Books International, Boston, 1982.
Illustration p. 11 (6, 7, 8) is from *Le Scienze Quaderni*, no 42, June 1988.
Illustration p. 20 is from *Quando l'uomo non c'era*, published by Fratelli Fabbri Editori, Milan, 1974.
Illustration p. 26 is from *Archosauria, A New Look at an Old Dinosaur*, published by The Viking Press, New York, 1979.

Graphics and Layout: The Graphics Department of Jaca Book.
Special thanks to the Museum of Natural History of Milan.

Printed and bound in the United States.

Contents

* The word billion is used throughout this book to mean one thousand million or 1 000 000 000.

The animal kingdom

When you are asked to think of an animal, what comes to mind? A dog, a cat, or maybe even an aardvark? In fact there are so many different kinds of animals that no-one can name them all.

Scientists have identified over one million different **species**, or types, of animals. But even this may be less than half the number of species that exist.

Animals great and small

Some species of animals are so tiny that they can only be seen through a microscope. Others, like whales, are very large. There is a whole world of animals in the soil. Animals swim through the water, fly through the air, and roam through grasslands, forests and deserts.

Evolution of animals

Billions of years ago there were very simple living things. Other more complicated living things evolved from these simple ones. As the Earth changes, species of living things continue to change, to fit in with their environment.

1 *Sponges (one of the simplest types of animal)*
2 *Snails and clams (mollusc)*
3 *A starfish (echinoderm)*
4 *A scorpion fish (bony fish)*
5 *A frog (amphibian)*
6 *A crocodile (reptile)*
7 *A pelican (bird)*
8 *A yak (mammal)*
9 *The chart shows the main lines of evolution in the animal kingdom.*

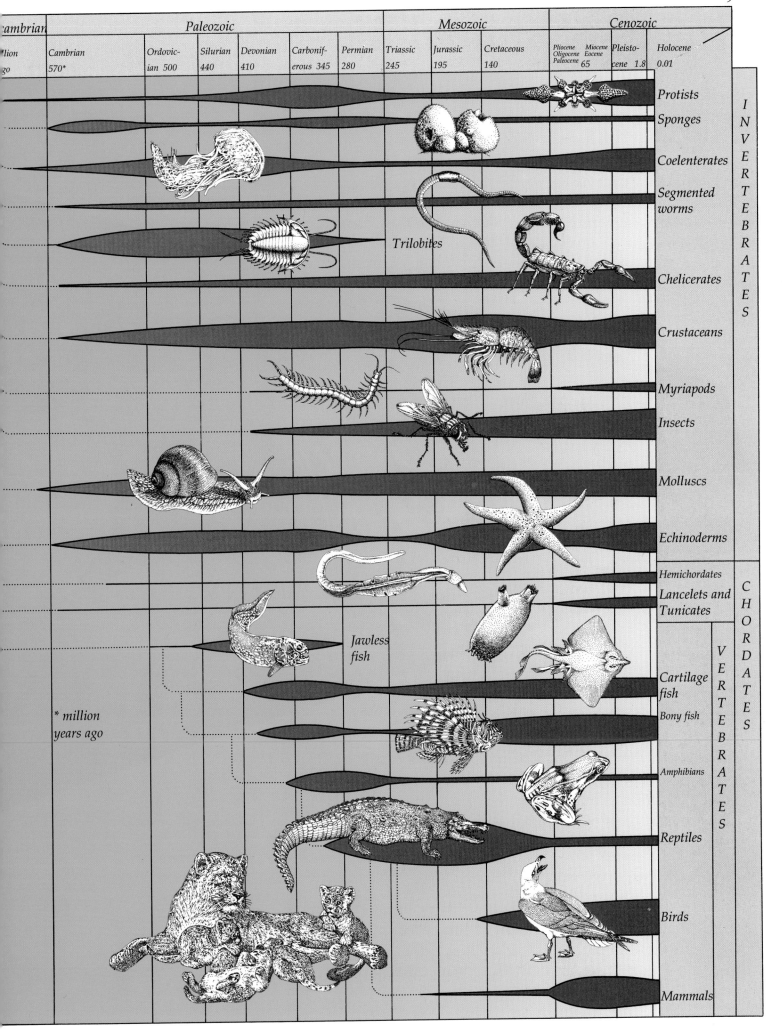

Traces of animal life

These illustrations are not drawn to scale.

To learn about **organisms** that lived millions of years ago, scientists study **fossils**, the remains or traces of once-living things which have been preserved. Usually when an animal or plant dies, it quickly decays.

Simple invertebrates: simple animals without backbones 630 million years ago

Protists: single-celled organisms 700 million years ago

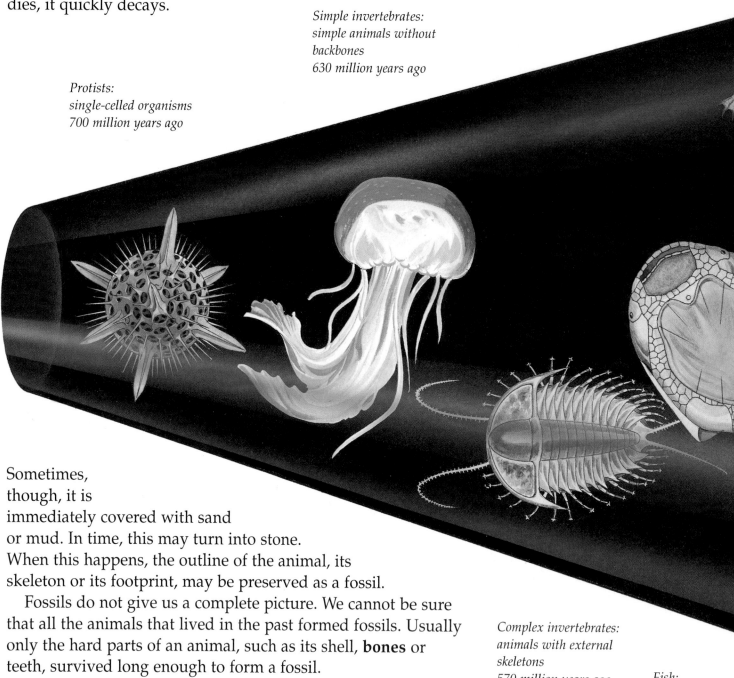

Sometimes, though, it is immediately covered with sand or mud. In time, this may turn into stone. When this happens, the outline of the animal, its skeleton or its footprint, may be preserved as a fossil.

Fossils do not give us a complete picture. We cannot be sure that all the animals that lived in the past formed fossils. Usually only the hard parts of an animal, such as its shell, **bones** or teeth, survived long enough to form a fossil.

Complex invertebrates: animals with external skeletons 570 million years ago

Fish: the first animals backbones 500 million years

Lines of evolution

Scientists have carefully worked out the basic lines of evolution. Animals evolved from very simple, single-celled organisms called protists. Simple animals without skeletons evolved from these. Later, fish, amphibians, reptiles, birds and **mammals** evolved.

Amphibians:
the first animals with
backbones to move out
of water
350 million years ago

Birds:
warm-blooded animals
that have feathers and
can fly
150 million years ago

Reptiles:
the first animals with backbones to
live entirely out of water
300 million years ago

Mammals:
warm-blooded animals that
suckle their young
220 million years ago

Life begins

The Earth was formed, along with the rest of the solar system, almost five billion years ago. In the beginning, the Earth was a fiery ball. Volcanoes erupted, releasing **water vapour** as well as poisonous gases. In time, as the Earth slowly cooled, pools of water formed.

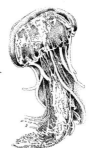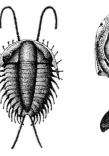

Simple invertebrates *Complex invertebrates*

Protists *Fish*

First living things evolve

Four billion years ago, the first, very simple, living things evolved. Scientists are not sure exactly how, but chemicals that were in the pools of water came together, and there was life.

At this time the Earth was still very hot. There was no **atmosphere** to protect the Earth from the ultraviolet rays from the Sun. Bacteria were one kind of organism which could survive in these conditions. Blue-green bacteria were especially important. They gave off **oxygen**, a gas needed by most living things. In time this oxygen formed the atmosphere, the layer of gases that surrounds and protects the Earth.

More complex living things develop

About seven hundred million years ago, bacteria evolved into more complex organisms called protists. The first protists were made up of only one **cell**, the smallest unit of living matter. But a protist's cell is complex since it has tiny structures inside it. One important structure is the **nucleus**, which directs all the activities within the cell.

1 *Scientists have tried to recreate the conditions in which life began. As life began in water, they have mixed gases and liquids which were probably present on Earth at that time, to make 'a primordial soup'. They added electric charges to provide energy. This combination produced amino acids and other substances. These are the basic matter of living cells.*

1

The first amino acids were formed in water.

Reptiles

Amphibians

Birds

Mammals

2 *For hundreds of millions of years the only changes that took place in living things were on a tiny scale. They took place within cells. The first cells were very simple and had no nucleus. Scientists think that different types of simple cells joined together and formed more complex cells. In the diagram below, the nucleus directs the activity of the cell; mitochondria produce energy; chloroplasts are important in photosynthesis; cilia are tiny and hair-like, and ciliates use them to help them move. The protists were cells like these. Protists evolved into both plants and animals.*

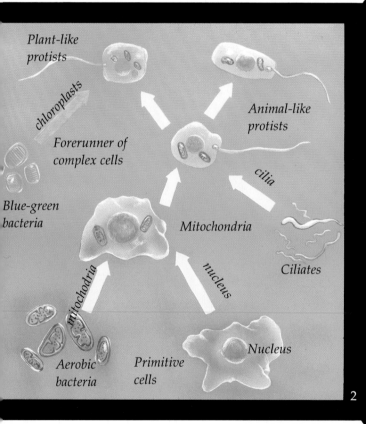

Plant-like protists

chloroplasts

Animal-like protists

Forerunner of complex cells

cilia

Blue-green bacteria

Mitochondria

mitochondria

Ciliates

nucleus

Aerobic bacteria

Primitive cells

Nucleus

2

3

4

3, 4 *Most protists have just one cell and are very small. These blocks of limestone were formed by the skeletons of millions of protists.*

Earliest animals

The animals which evolved from the protists had soft bodies and did not have bones or shells. Animals like this are called **invertebrates**. They had no hard parts that could easily form fossils. However, in 1947, scientists found fossils of one of the earliest animals – a jellyfish.

Jellyfish

The small jellyfish fossils the scientists found are from the Precambrian Period and are at least 630 million years old. Some types of these early jellyfish and their relatives lived attached to the ocean floor. Others crawled on the muddy bottom, and some swam through the water. Animals related to these early forms can still be found today, usually in warm ocean waters.

Jellyfish are shaped like parachutes, with long tentacles. The jellyfish uses the tentacles to catch small animals that live in the water. There are stinging cells on the tentacles – these stun the prey. These cells give off a poison. In some cases it is strong enough to injure, or even kill, people.

Other soft-bodied animals

There were other soft-bodied animals in the ocean millions of years ago. Some were sponges, very simple animals that live attached to the ocean bottom. Sponges feed by pulling water through their bodies and filtering out tiny bits of food.

There were also several types of worm. The segmented worm was the most complex type. This is a distant ancestor of the earthworm you can find in your garden. But there were probably many other animals unknown to us. These animals either evolved or died out hundreds of millions of years ago.

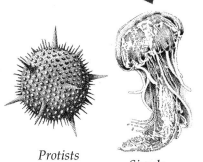
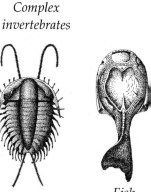

Protists

Simple invertebrates

Complex invertebrates

Fish

1

2

2 *This is how the Australian seafloor might have looked during the Precambrian time. The things which look like fern leaves are actually a type of soft-bodied coral that is now extinct.*

3, 4, 5 *These fossils of simple invertebrates were found in South Australia: Spriggina floundersi, a segmented worm; Dickinsonia costata, another extinct worm; and Charniodiscus oppositus.*

6, 7, 8 *Animals of today related to these fossils: Tomopteris longisetis, Sphinter citrinus and Pennatula rubra.*

1 *Remains of Reticulomedusa greenei, a typical jellyfish of the Carboniferous Period.*

Amphibians   Reptiles   Birds   Mammals

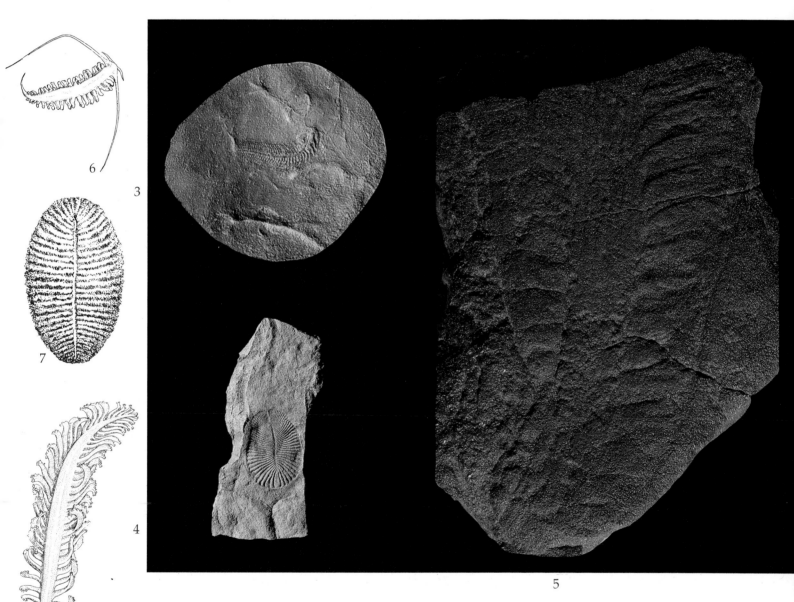

3
4
5
6
7
8

On pages 16 and 17 you can see how the bottom of the sea might have looked. This is based on an area of British Columbia, Canada, which is famous for its fossils. We can see: Anomalocaris, that swam like a devil fish; Odontogriphus, a simple flatworm; Opabinia, with five eyes and a mouth like an elephant's trunk; Wiwaxia, with scales and long stickers; Marrella, with a wedge-shaped head and four large horn-shaped stingers; Pikaia, the oldest-known ancestor of the vertebrates; Canadia, with huge feathered gills; Aysheaia, climbing up on a sponge; three Dinomischus, strange animals that look like daisies. Finally, in a den dug into the mud, the Ottoia.

Opabinia   *Odontogriphus (above)*   *Wiwaxia (above)*   *Marrella*

Pikaia

Aysheaia

Dinomischus

Canadia

Ottoia

17

Animals with hard coverings or shells

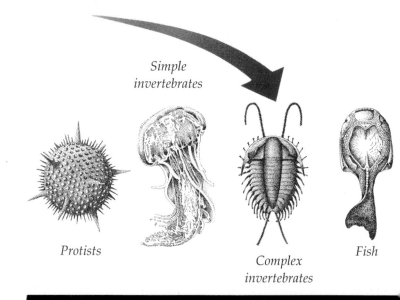

Simple invertebrates

Protists

Complex invertebrates

Fish

During the Cambrian Period, over 500 million years ago, there was an explosion of evolution and many new species appeared. Suddenly the seas were filled with a variety of animals. Some had hard body coverings or shells. These are complex invertebrates.

Animals that build islands

Coral is an animal which attaches itself to a surface and forms a shell around its body. The coral's young attach themselves to the shell of the older coral. In time huge mounds build up. These can get so large that they form reefs or islands in the ocean.

Animals with one or two shells

Other animals with shells are the **molluscs**, which usually have one or two shells. You will have seen molluscs living today, such as snails or clams. A clam pulls water between its shells and into its body. From the water, the clam filters out tiny bits of food. In this way it also gets the oxygen it needs and gets rid of carbon dioxide.

Animals with segmented bodies

You may have seen some crustaceans we know today, such as shrimp and crayfish. These animals are one type of arthropod, animals with segmented bodies and jointed legs. An **exoskeleton**, or skeleton on the outside of the body, forms a hard, protective covering. Today there are more species of arthropods than of all other animals combined. Trilobites were the most common arthropod for millions of years – they are now extinct.

1 These are Basidechenella rowi, examples of trilobites from the Devonian Period. Trilobites had a protective shell in three parts. They had many pairs of legs on the underside of their bodies.

1

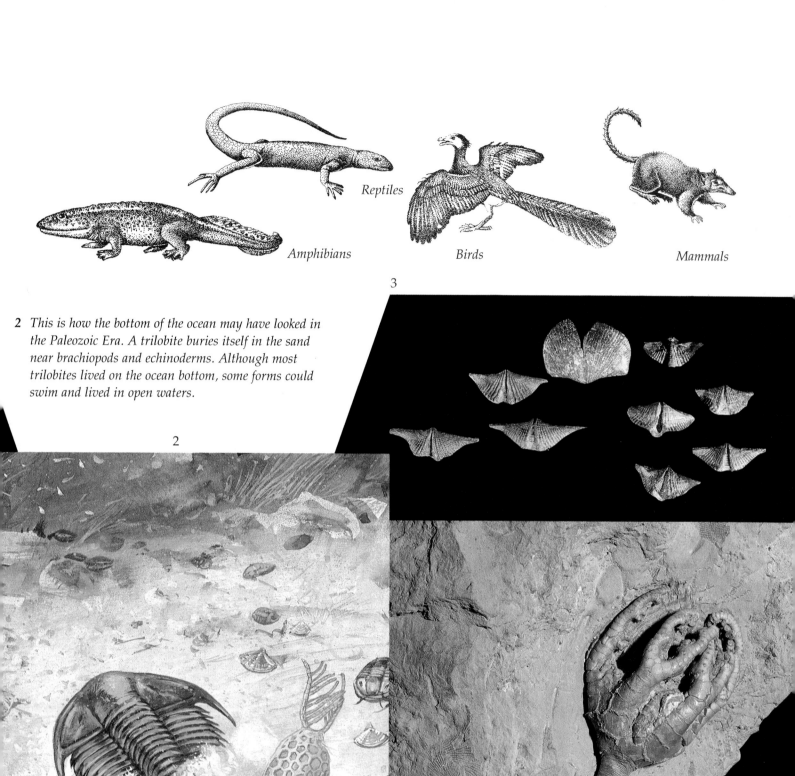

Reptiles

Amphibians

Birds

Mammals

3

2 This is how the bottom of the ocean may have looked in the Paleozoic Era. A trilobite buries itself in the sand near brachiopods and echinoderms. Although most trilobites lived on the ocean bottom, some forms could swim and lived in open waters.

2

3 Brachiopods are animals that look like, but are not related to, molluscs. These brachiopods lived during the Devonian Period.

4 This fossil of Onychocrinus exculptus is from the Carboniferous Period. It is related to modern echinoderms, a group of species which include animals such as the starfish and sea urchin.

4

Animals with backbones

The exoskeleton of an arthropod has to be shed as the animal grows. It was a major evolutionary change when some species of animals evolved a skeleton inside the body. Muscles were attached to this internal skeleton which provided support for the whole body. This system of internal skeleton and muscles evolved in time to give animals strength and fast movement.

With or without a backbone?

Animals with an internal skeleton are called **vertebrates**. Most animal species do not have internal skeletons, so they are invertebrates.

Vertebrates evolve

Vertebrates evolved from invertebrates about 500 million years ago. The oldest vertebrate fossils that have been found date from around that time.

Jawless fish appear

The first vertebrates were very primitive fish called **agnathans**, which have almost completely died out. Unlike most fish found now, the agnathans have no jaw. Today, fish like these feed by attaching themselves to other fish and sucking out food. The first agnathans probably sucked up mud and filtered out bits of food. Scientists think that agnathans did not evolve in the sea. Instead they probably appeared first in freshwater lakes or in the salt water of river **deltas** where rivers empty into the sea.

The earliest and most primitive agnathans were called ostracoderms. These small fish had snakelike tails and large heads encased in shells made up of bony plates. They were probably very poor swimmers. They were weighted down by their heavy, plated heads and also had very small fins.

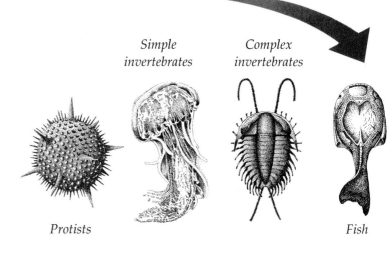

Simple invertebrates *Complex invertebrates*

Protists *Fish*

1 *This invertebrate has a shell covering its soft body.*
2 *Scientists do not know much about the early evolution of vertebrates. One problem is that very few early vertebrate fossils have been found. Early examples are needed to see how they evolved from the invertebrates. Some scientists think they may have evolved from a group of echinoderms that lived from the Cambrian to the Devonian Periods. Today's echinoderms, such as the starfish and sea anenomes, have circular body plans. Those which may be the ancestors of vertebrates had a left and right side, a fat body covered with plates, and a tail.*
3 *This fish also has a bony covering but its internal skeleton is what shows it is a vertebrate.*

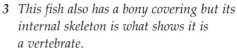

covering m... up of bony plates

internal cartilage skeleton

soft parts

spinal column

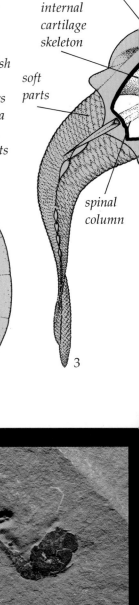

shell – the external skeleton of a chitin

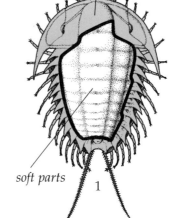

soft parts

1

2

3

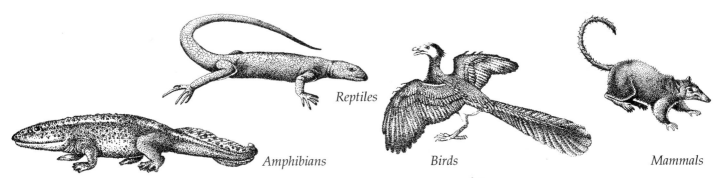

Amphibians
Reptiles
Birds
Mammals

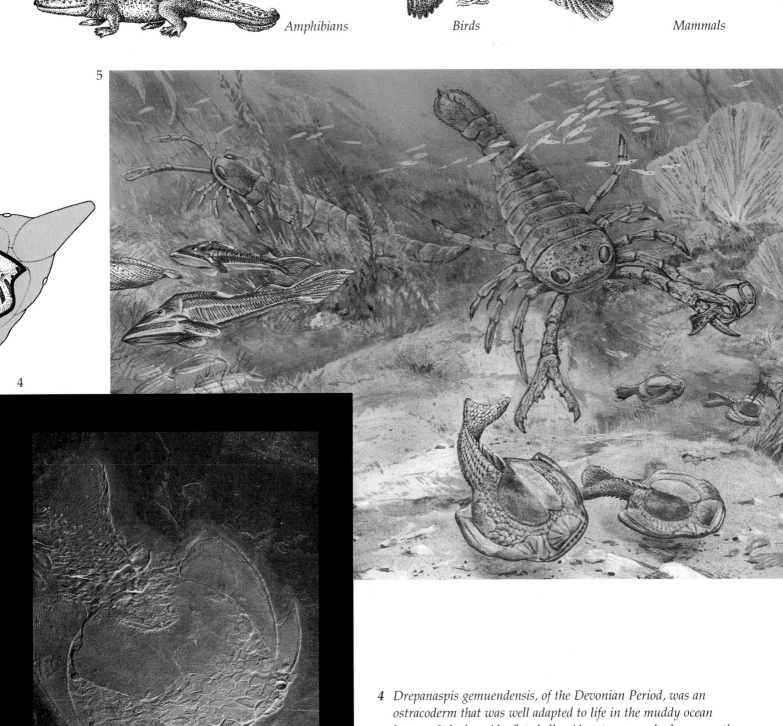

4 Drepanaspis gemuendensis, of the Devonian Period, was an ostracoderm that was well adapted to life in the muddy ocean bottom. It had a wide, flat shell, wide-set eyes, and a large mouth.

5 During the Silurian Period, about 400 million years ago, different types of ostracoderms could be found in the ocean. But the invertebrates still ruled the seas. Here the sea scorpion on the right is about to attack a Drepanaspis, whose only protection is its hard shell. On the left are examples of Hemicyclaspis, another ostracoderm.

The kingdom of fish

About 400 million years ago, during the Devonian Period, many different kinds of fish evolved. Some were different species of placoderms. These were types of ostracoderm. Some of them grew to almost 10 metres in length.

Skeletons from cartilage

Two main lines of fish which evolved from the placoderms are still found today. One line includes sharks, rays and skates. These fish have internal skeletons that are made up of **cartilage**. Your nose is made of cartilage. This means it is flexible – try wiggling it! Because they have changed so little for millions of years, sharks are sometimes referred to as 'living fossils'.

Skeletons from bone

The other line of placoderms evolved into fish with skeletons made of bone. Most of the fish we know today fit into this large group of bony fish. One feature of bony fish is a swim bladder. The swim bladder is a gas-filled sac inside the fish's body that helps the fish swim. When the bladder is filled with air, the fish rises in the water. When gas is let out, the fish goes deeper in the water.

By the end of the Devonian Period, the bony fish had evolved into two more lines. One line led to the development of modern bony fish and lived in cold and deep seas. The other line lived in fresh and warm water and evolved into amphibians – vertebrates that could live out of water.

1 *This fossil shows the Cyclobatis, a type of ray, or broad flat fish. It dates from the upper Cretaceous Period.*

2 *A typical placoderm can be seen here. This fossil of Bothriolepis canadensis dates from the upper Devonian Period. The head, front flippers and part of the body are covered with a strong shell of bony plates. There was only one small opening for the eyes and nostrils.*

1

3 *The large shark to which this tooth belonged lived about 20 million years ago.*

4 *This shark was about 40 centimetres long and lived during the Cretaceous Period. Even the soft body parts are perfectly preserved in this fossil.*

5 *This is a fossil of Mene rhombea, a bony fish that lived in tropical waters.*

6 *This diagram shows the evolution of fish. The numbers on the left indicate millions of years, so the earliest types of fish are shown at the bottom.*

2

3

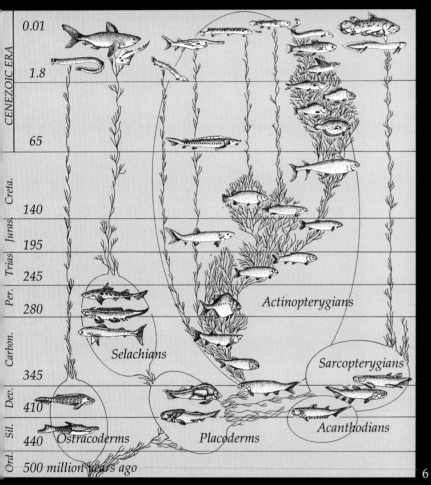

CENEZOIC ERA	0.01	
	1.8	
	65	
Creta.	140	
Juras.	195	
Trias.	245	
Per.	280	Actinopterygians
Carbon.	345	
		Selachians
		Sarcopterygians
Dev.	410	
Sil.	440	Acanthodians
		Ostracoderms
Ord.	500 million years ago	Placoderms

6

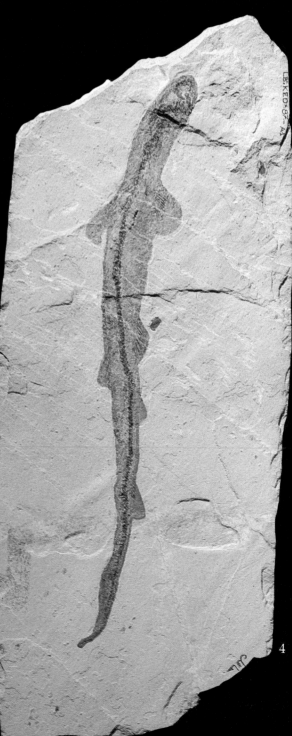

4

5

Animals move on to land

Animals and plants only existed in water until the end of the Silurian Period, over 400 million years ago. Then the first plants evolved along the damp banks of the water. Soon after that, invertebrates also appeared on land.

Early land dwellers

Centipedes are arthropods that look a little like segmented worms. They were one of the first animal groups on land. Other arthropods, such as early scorpions and huge dragonflies, also lived on land. About 50 million years later, the first vertebrates appeared.

Amphibians begin to evolve

Most fish breathe through gills. Water flows through the gills, and the oxygen which is dissolved in the water is absorbed into the body. In some fish an additional organ developed. The swim bladders in some bony fishes evolved into simple lungs. These fish no longer depended only on oxygen dissolved in water – they could also take in oxygen from the air.

Around 400 million years ago, the **climate** was changing and there were long periods of drought. Swamps dried up. Those fish that could breathe through lungs as well as gills were able to survive until the rains came again.

The fins of some of these fish were strong. They could move the animal over land, not just through the water. With flipper-like limbs and lungs these fish were evolving into amphibians, animals that could live both in water and on land.

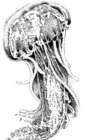  

Simple invertebrates *Complex invertebrates*

Protists *Fish*

1 *This is what a forest in the Carboniferous Period might have looked like. Notice the giant dragonfly and a scorpion. The warm and damp environment encouraged the development of amphibians.*

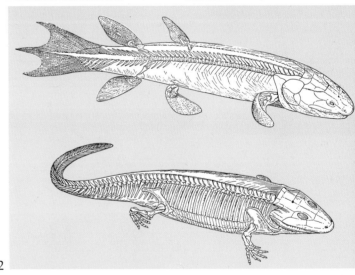

2 *The fish at the top is Eusthenopteron, a bony fish of the Devonian Period. Below it is Ichthyostega, an amphibian of the Carboniferous Period.*

3 *A dragonfly of the Cretaceous Period. Arthropods were the first animals to fly.*
4 *Another bony fish of the Devonian Period, Osteolepis. It is similar to Eusthenopteron in 2.*
5 *A fossil of an amphibian of the Permian Period, called Sclerocephalus. There is the tail of a fish under its head and to the left.*

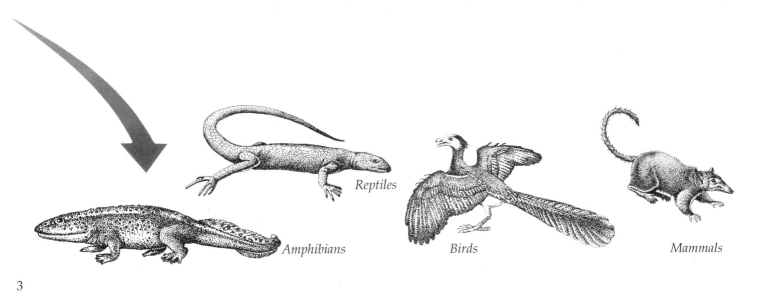

Amphibians

Reptiles

Birds

Mammals

3

4

5

25

The arrival of reptiles

Amphibians depend on water. Although most of them do not need to be in water all the time, they still spend part of their lives there. Young amphibians grow from egg to adult in water. Most adult amphibians live on land but they must still return to the water to lay their delicate, jellylike eggs. Unlike a chicken's egg, with its hard shell, the amphibian's egg has no shell and can dry out quickly.

The climate warms up

Around 300 million years ago, the climate of many areas of the Earth became warmer. Small pools of water began to dry up and did not refill during a rainy season. As a result, animals that did not need to spend part of their lives in water were more successful. This was particularly true at the edge of warm, humid forests, where the climate was very unstable.

Reptiles live out of water

Some animals evolved that laid eggs with thick, leathery shells. Inside the shell the **embryo** was in a watery environment where it had food and oxygen. It was just as if it had been laid in a tiny, protected pool of water. The adults that grew from these eggs had a thick skin that would not easily dry out. These newly evolved animals were reptiles, vertebrates that could live their entire lives out of water.

Cotylosaur reptiles were the first true land reptiles. They were not in danger of drying out in the warmer climate because the adults were covered with hard scales, and their eggs had leathery shells.

This shows how two reptiles may have looked during the Permian Period. The one on the right, Scutosaurus, eats plants and has just laid its eggs. On the left, the meat-eating Phthinosuchus is ready to attack.

The inset picture shows a reptile's egg. The embryo is surrounded by liquid. The orange tissue supplies food; the brown tissue supplies oxygen.

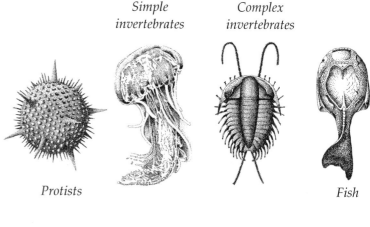

Simple invertebrates   Complex invertebrates

Protists   Fish

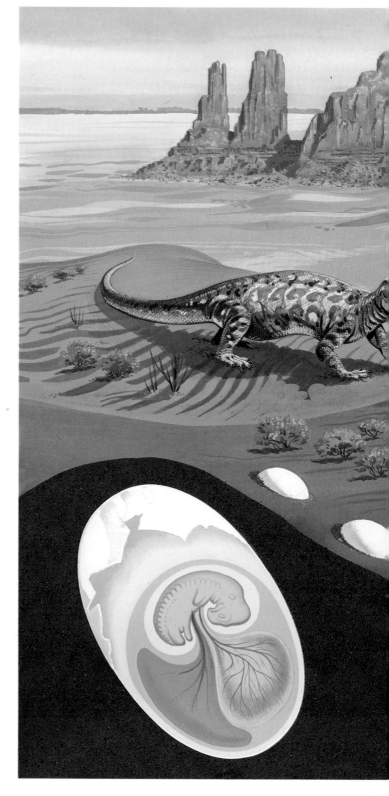

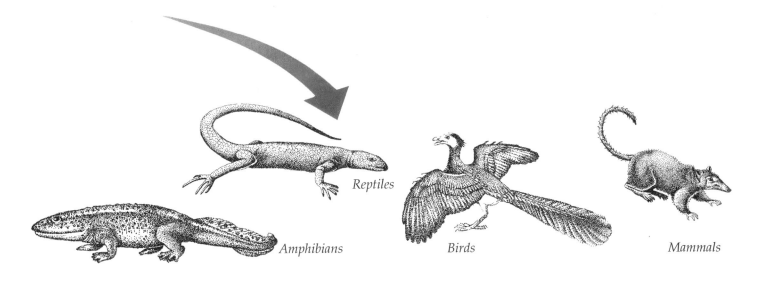

Amphibians *Reptiles* *Birds* *Mammals*

Reptiles everywhere

The climate remained dry and warm until the end of the Paleozoic Era, over 200 million years ago. The wet areas where amphibians lived dried up and many amphibians died out. These conditions were perfect for reptiles, however, and they continued to evolve. Reptiles adapted to their surroundings. They prowled on land, swam in the water, and flew through the air. Reptiles were the dominant animals of the Mesozoic Era.

Reptiles which swam

Some reptiles returned to the water and lived alongside their distant ancestors, the fish. Reptiles with flippers and streamlined bodies adapted best to life in the water. However, they still breathed through lungs. The most spectacular examples of these reptiles were the ichthyosaurs and the plesiosaurs.

Reptiles which flew

The first vertebrates that could fly were reptiles – the **pterosaurs**. These reptiles were much lighter than their ancestors. Wing membranes helped them glide through the air.

1 *This chart shows the evolution of dinosaurs.*

1	*Cotylosaurs*	*9*	*Rhynchocephalia*	*19*	*Theropods*
2	*Protosaurs*	*10*	*Stegosaurs*	*20*	*Sauropods*
3	*Nothosaurs*	*11*	*Ankylosaurs*	*21*	*Anfichelidi*
4	*Plesiosaurs*	*12*	*Ceratopsia*	*22*	*Pleurodira*
5	*Placodonts*	*13*	*Ornithopods*	*23*	*Criptodiri*
6	*Ophidians*	*14*	*Thecodonts*	*24*	*Ichthyosaurs*
7	*Saurians*	*15*	*Ranforinchi*	*25*	*Mesosaurs*
8	*Eosuchia*	*16*	*Pterodactyls*	*26*	*Plycosaurs*
		17	*Mesosuchia*	*27*	*Therapsids*
		18	*Eusuchia*		

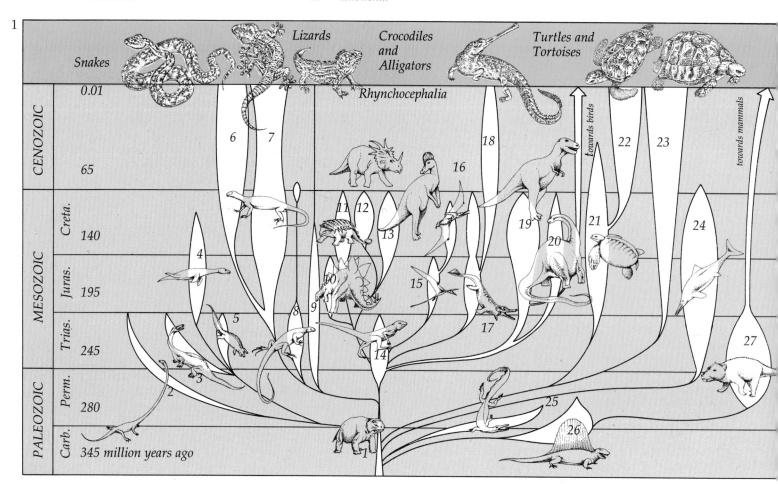

2 This pterosaur was the earliest flying reptile, dating from the Triassic Period. It was about 30 centimetres long and had a wing span of over one metre.

3 A skeleton of Bradysaurus baini of the Permian Period. It lived in very dry areas.

4 Neusticosaurus edwardsi, a reptile of the Triassic Period which lived in coastal sea waters.

5 The reptiles best suited to swimming were the ichthyosaurs. They were the same shape as a dolphin. This Stenopterygius quadriscissus dates from the Jurassic Period.

The age of dinosaurs

Dinosaurs were the reptiles which ruled the land. The legs of early reptiles were at the sides, and this made them walk with a waddle. Later, dinosaurs evolved so that their legs were beneath their bodies. Their legs held them up so they could walk upright. Dinosaurs with this new body plan could move quickly.

2

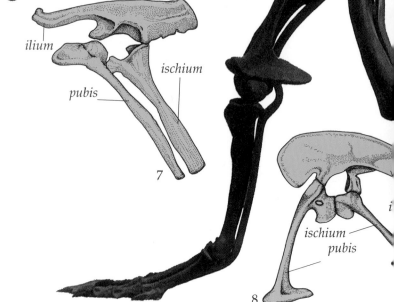

1

6

They could grow very large. Some were more than 30 metres long. Others were smaller. One of the earliest species was about the size of a chicken.

All kinds of dinosaurs

A great variety of dinosaurs developed. Some were herbivores, that ate only plants; others were carnivores, that ate meat – including other dinosaurs. Some dinosaurs were tiny and could run almost as fast as racehorses. Some ran fast to catch their prey; others ran fast to escape. Generally, the good runners ran on their hind legs. Many dinosaurs were covered by bony plates, large horns, or sharp spines. For 140 million years this varied group of reptiles ruled the Earth.

ilium

ischium

pubis

7

ischium
pubis

i

8

1   *Skeleton of Allosaurus fragilis. Its upright walk and sharp teeth and claws made this dinosaur one of North America's best hunters in the Jurassic Period.*

2   *Skull of Parasaurolophus. This was a duck-billed dinosaur of the Cretaceous Period. Its small, even teeth suggest that it ate plants.*

3   *Imprint of Anchisauripus, Triassic Period.*

4   *Eggs of Protoceratops, Cretaceous Period.*

5   *Teeth of Tarbosaurus, Cretaceous Period.*

6   *Compare the bone structure of the dinosaurs and other reptiles. In most reptiles (left) the legs were at the side of the body. In dinosaurs (right) the legs were directly under the animal.*

7, 8   *On the basis of a different arrangement of bones we can identify two main groups of dinosaur: ornithischians (7) and saurischians (8).*

9   *Different types of dinosaurs.*

Brachiosaurus

Corythosaurus

Chasmosaurus

9

Stegosaurus

Plateosaurus

Homocephale

The beginning of birds

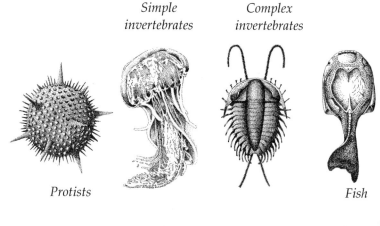

Simple invertebrates   *Complex invertebrates*

Protists   *Fish*

Birds began to evolve during the time of the dinosaurs. Over one hundred years ago traces of an early bird species, Archaeopterix, were found along with dinosaur bones in a quarry in Europe.

Dinosaurs evolve into birds

Over millions of years some dinosaur species gradually changed. Scientists believe that one line of dinosaurs, that lived in the trees, evolved into birds. They developed into animals that were well-adapted for flight. Their front limbs evolved into wings. They developed feathers, and their bodies were lighter.

Birds of today are quite different from their reptile ancestors. They have hollow bones and no teeth. This makes the animal very light for its size. It also means a bird does not have to use much energy to get airborne. Wings and feathers are also light, helping the bird get into the air and stay in flight.

The earliest bird

We can tell from the fossil that Archaeopterix was not very good at flying. However, it was probably good at gliding. It could climb up trees in search of the insects it ate and would then sail from branch to branch or down to the ground.

Archaeopterix lived about 150 million years ago, during the upper Jurassic Period. Other birds evolved from this first bird. Most present-day birds had evolved by about 140 million years ago.

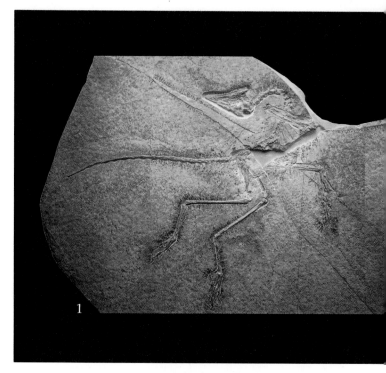

1, 2 These limestone slabs from the upper Jurassic Period open up like a book to reveal a specimen of Archaeopteryx lithographica, the earliest known bird.

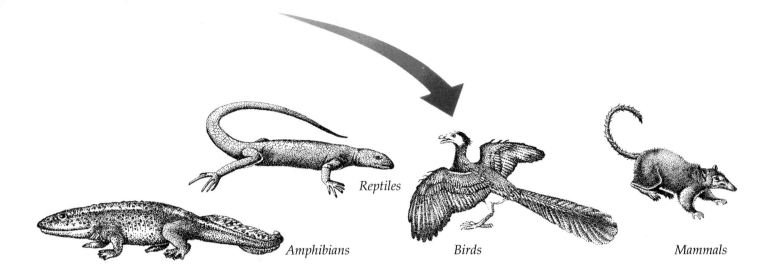

Reptiles

Amphibians

Birds

Mammals

2

3

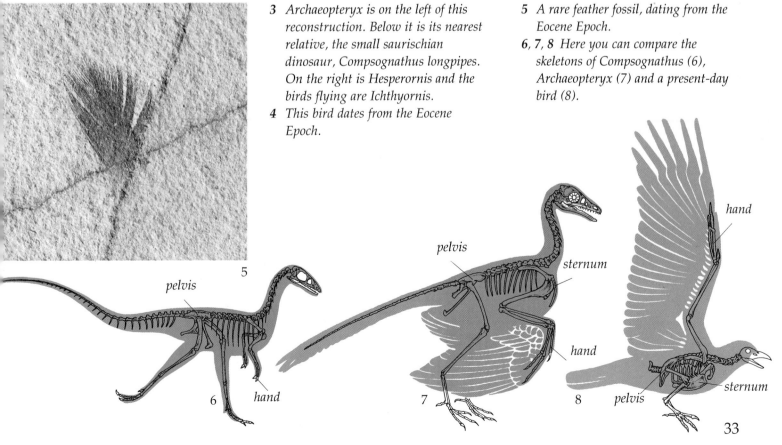

3 Archaeopteryx is on the left of this
reconstruction. Below it is its nearest
relative, the small saurischian
dinosaur, Compsognathus longpipes.
On the right is Hesperornis and the
birds flying are Ichthyornis.
4 This bird dates from the Eocene
Epoch.

5 A rare feather fossil, dating from the
Eocene Epoch.
6, 7, 8 Here you can compare the
skeletons of Compsognathus (6),
Archaeopteryx (7) and a present-day
bird (8).

5

pelvis

pelvis

sternum

hand

hand

pelvis

sternum

6

hand

7

8

33

The first mammals

Before the appearance of dinosaurs, one group of reptiles was evolving in a way that was different from most of the others. This group was called the therapsids. Like the dinosaurs it evolved a new body plan. Its legs grew directly under the body. This allowed the animal to move quickly and easily. The therapsids had teeth of different sizes, allowing them to eat various types of food.

Controlling body heat

Most reptiles depended on their surroundings to warm and cool their bodies, but therapsids could control their own body heat. Some therapsids cooled their bodies with the help of large sail-like structures on their backs. When they were too hot, blood would flow through the 'sail' and be cooled. Once they had cooled down, less blood would move through this structure. Later therapsids had hair on their bodies. This helped to keep them warm.

Feeding the young

Some therapsids evolved into mammals. Like mammals they had hair or fur and teeth of different sizes. At some time, mammals also evolved the feature that gives them their name – the mammary, or milk gland. Female mammals, unlike all other animals, feed their young milk from the mammary glands.

Small and furry mammals

These first mammals were very small and furry, rather like the shrews of today. With their fur to keep them warm, they could stay active at night. This meant they could feed on small plants and insects while the dinosaurs slept. These first mammals laid eggs.

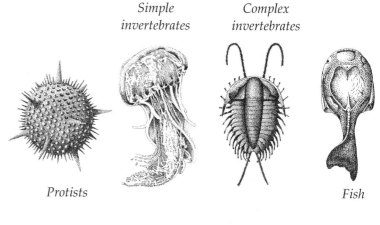

Simple invertebrates *Complex invertebrates*

Protists *Fish*

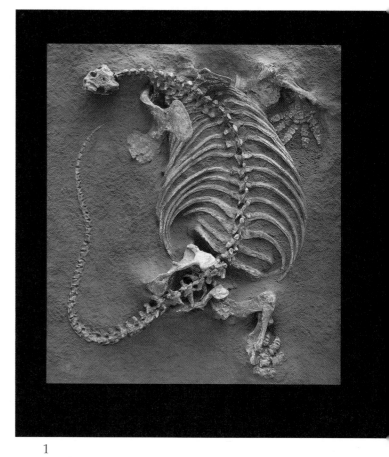

1

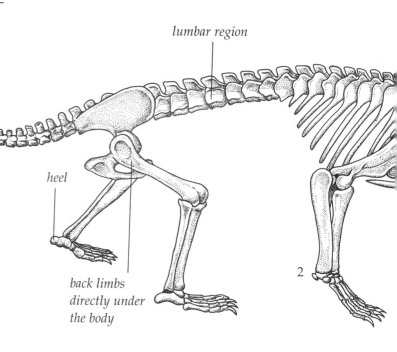

lumbar region

heel

back limbs directly under the body

2

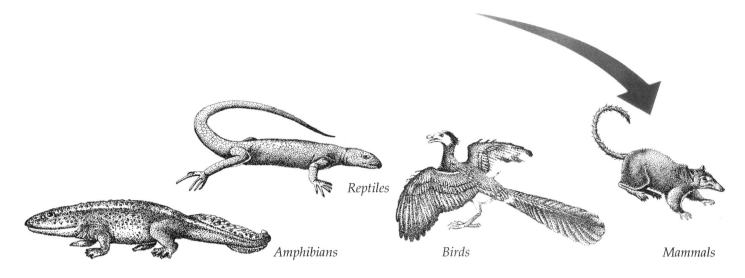

Amphibians   Reptiles   Birds   Mammals

frontal eyes

one-piece jaw

paired canine teeth

3

1 Therapsids descended from reptiles like this of the Permian Period, Catylorhynchus romeri. These early reptiles were the first to control their body heat.

2 The skeleton of this therapsid, Thrinaxodon, is very similar to a mammal's. Notice the jaw made up of one bone. In other reptiles the jaw is made up of several bones.

3 The Sun is setting 200 million years ago. The mammals of the Mesozoic Era found night time the safest time to search for food. Here two small Morganucodon are hidden in the bushes.

Extinction of the dinosaurs

Evolution is usually a slow and gradual process. However, sudden events can have a dramatic effect on evolution. Entire groups of animals have disappeared from the Earth in relatively short periods of time.

Species vanish

One sudden event was the extinction, or dying out, of species at the end of the Paleozoic Era. Trilobites were one of the most common groups of animals at the time. They vanished, along with many other species. The best known extinction is that of the dinosaurs 65 million years ago. Many other reptiles, including ichthyosaurs, plesiosaurs and pterosaurs, disappeared at the same time.

Possible reasons

Scientists are not sure why so many species of animals died out at this time. Some suggest that there may have been a sudden change in the climate. If the climate suddenly became much colder, for example, many plants would not survive. Animals cannot live without plants. Even those that eat meat depend on plants as food for their prey.

Some scientists think that the extinction of the dinosaurs was caused by a huge **meteorite** hitting the Earth. Meteorites, or rocks flying through space, do not often hit the Earth's surface – they usually burn up in the atmosphere. If a large meteorite did land on Earth, it could fill the sky with dust and block out the Sun's light. This would cause the death of many plants, and the animals that depend on them would not be able to survive.

1 *This is what might have happened. The impact of a meteorite would cover the Earth with dust and debris, making it impossible for plants and animals to survive.*
2 *Ammonites, extinct types of molluscs, were one of the many groups of animal species that died out along with the dinosaurs.*

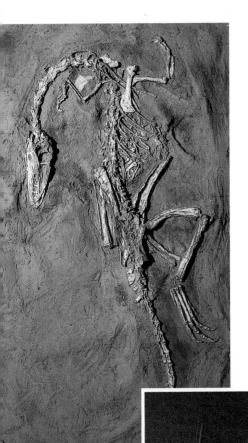

3 *Coelophysis bauri was a small agile dinosaur of the upper Triassic Period. It may have been a cannibal as it has a young dinosaur of its own species in its stomach. Its neck is bent back because its tendons tightened after death.*

3

4

5

6

4, 5, 6 Today we can only see dinosaurs in museums. This large, meat-eating Tarbosaurus bataar dates from the upper Cretaceous Period and was dug up in 1985 in Mongolia. Scientists think it is the Asian cousin of the North American Tyrannosaurus.

The age of mammals

The first mammals evolved at the time of the dinosaurs. But the event that killed the dinosaurs did not destroy mammals. For 150 million years the giant reptiles had ruled the Earth. Now the mammals could finally flourish.

All kinds of mammals

Mammals first appeared as small animals, but they now evolved into all kinds of different sizes and shapes. During the Eocene Epoch, 50 million years ago, there were mammals in the sky and water, and on land. Bats flew through the air, and whales and dolphins swam in the ocean, while a tremendous variety of mammals moved over the land. All the mammals which exist today developed from these early mammals.

Reasons for success

The first reason for the success of mammals is that they can control their body heat. This means that they can adjust to changing conditions. They can survive in the heat of the plains or the cool of a forest.

The second reason is just as important. Most mammals do not lay eggs. Instead they give birth to well-developed young. Mammals care for their young, making it more likely that their young will survive and continue the species.

1

1   Skull of Bison priscus, a bison that lived in Europe at the end of the Pleistocene Epoch.
2   Skull of Ursus spelaeus, a bear from the Pleistocene Epoch.
3   Skull of Merycoidodon, Oligocene Epoch. Scientists think it is an ancestor of cattle, but it has long sharp teeth.
4   Detail of the skeleton of Paroodectes feisti, a typical species from the Eocene Epoch.
5   Elephas falconeri, Pleistocene Epoch. Only 90 centimetres tall when full-grown, it was the smallest elephant of all time.
6   Skeleton of a sirenian, a sea mammal from the Cenozoic Era.
7   Megaloceros hibernicus, Pleistocene Epoch. The horns of this gigantic stag spread more than three metres wide.
8   Elephas primigenius, better known as a woolly mammoth, was an enormous elephant that lived in Europe and Asia during the last Ice Age.
9   Skeleton of Gomphotherium, a strange elephant of the Miocene Epoch. It had two pairs of tusks that curved downwards.
10 Fossil of a bat of the genus Archaeonycteris from the Eocene Epoch.
11 Chart showing the evolution of mammals.

5   6   7

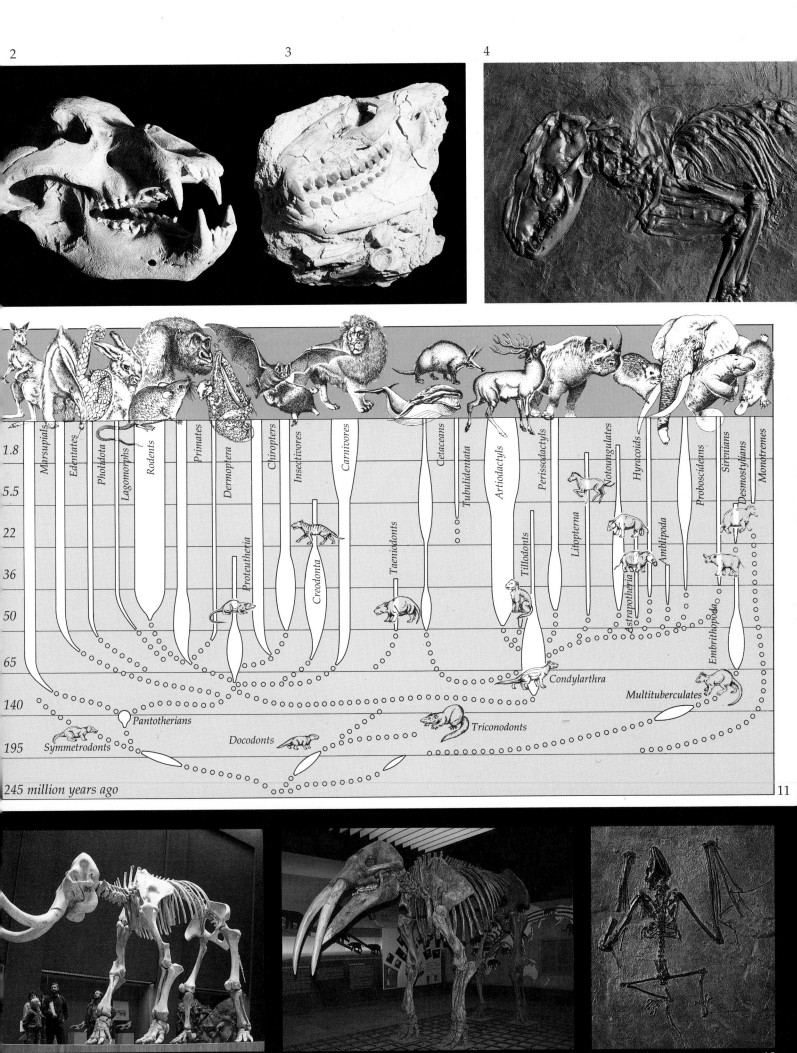

1.8
5.5
22
36
50
65
140
195
245 million years ago

Marsupials
Edentates
Pholidota
Lagomorphs
Rodents
Primates
Proteutheria
Dermoptera
Chiropters
Insectivores
Creodonta
Carnivores
Taeniodonts
Cetaceans
Tubulidentata
Artiodactyls
Tillodonts
Perissodactyls
Litopterna
Notoungulates
Astrapotheria
Amblipoda
Hyracoids
Embrithopoda
Proboscideans
Sirenians
Desmostylians
Monotremes

Condylarthra
Multituberculates
Pantotherians
Triconodonts
Docodonts
Symmetrodonts

2
3
4
8
9
10
11

1 In this drawing of a grassland from the Pleistocene Epoch, a sabre-
  toothed tiger attacks a zebra. This species of tiger was a very
  successful carnivore at one time. It is now extinct.
  An animal is successful that adapts well to its environment. But
  environments change. There have been ice ages and long droughts.
  If an animal species is to survive, it must adapt to the changing
  environment. It may change so much that it evolves into a different
  species. But if it is unable to adapt, it will become extinct.
2 Skull of Smilodon californicus, a sabre-toothed tiger that lived in
  North America until the end of the Pleistocene Epoch.

2

3 *These chimpanzees are living in a zoo. Their life is as natural*
as possible. They are close relatives of humans. Like humans,
they can use tools. Like humans, they live in family groups
and care for their young. Scientists study chimpanzees to
learn more about their own ancestors.
Increasing our knowledge of all animal species is important
because as humans we affect so many other living things.
Humans have the ability to change the environment. When the
environment changes all living things are affected. Only if
humans are aware of all animals and their needs will the
safety, and even survival, of other animals be assured.

Glossary

agnathans: jawless fish. The first type of fish. This group has only a few surviving members.

amino acids: organic compounds that make up the basic structure of proteins (see page 12).

atmosphere: the gases that surround the Earth.

bone: a stiff support tissue, rich in calcium, that makes up the skeleton of most vertebrates.

brachiopods: sea molluscs with two shells, such as clams and mussels (see page 19).

cartilage: a flexible supporting tissue that makes up the skeleton of the most primitive groups of vertebrates. It is also found in some parts of more complex vertebrates, such as in the nose and ear of humans.

cell: the basic unit of all living things.

chitin: organic material that makes up the shell of some invertebrates, such as trilobites, crustaceans, and insects (see page 20).

climate: the typical weather in an area.

cotylosaurs: an extinct, primitive order of reptiles with squat bodies and short legs. They are believed to be the first reptiles.

delta: an accumulation of sediments at the mouth of a river where it enters a lake or the ocean.

embryo: the earliest stage in the development of an organism.

exoskeleton: an external skeleton, typical of many invertebrates.

fossils: the remains, traces, and imprints of organisms that lived in the past and that have been preserved.

invertebrate: an animal without an internal skeleton. It may have an external skeleton or a soft body.

mammals: a group of warm-blooded vertebrates that have hair and suckle their young.

meteorite: an extra-terrestrial object that falls to the Earth's surface from space.

mollusc: a soft-bodied animal usually covered by a shell. Examples include snails and slugs.

nucleus: the part of a cell which directs its activities.

organism: a living thing, either animal or plant.

ornithischians: an order of dinosaurs with a pelvis whose pubic bone is turned backward, as it is in birds (see page 31).

oxygen: an odourless and colourless gas found in air and water and needed by most living things.

pterosaurs: an extinct order of reptiles. Their front limbs, similar to those of bats, were adapted into wings, which were formed by a thin membrane, or layer of skin. This thin membrane was held by the very long fourth finger of the hand and joined to the body and to the back limbs.

saurischians: an order of dinosaurs that have a pelvis whose pubic bone is turned forward, as in the case of many present-day reptiles (see page 31).

species: the smallest classification group for organisms, for example red squirrels (*Sciurus vulgaris*) and grey squirrels (*Sciurus carolinensis*) are different species.

sternum: the breastbone of vertebrates.

vertebrates: animals with a backbone. The word vertebrate comes from the name of the bones that make up the backbone.

water vapour: water in a gaseous state.

Index

Numbers in **bold** refer to illustrations.

EVOLUTION OF THE MONERAN, PROTIST, PLANT, AND FUNGI KINGDOMS

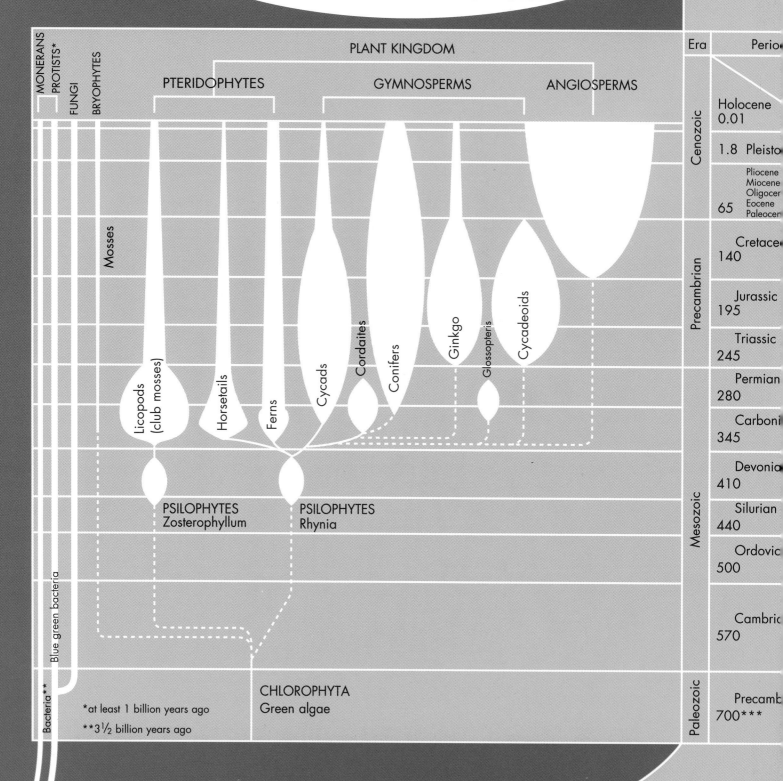

MONERANS
PROTISTS*
FUNGI
BRYOPHYTES

PLANT KINGDOM

PTERIDOPHYTES   GYMNOSPERMS   ANGIOSPERMS

Mosses

Licopods (club mosses)

Horsetails

Ferns

Cycads

Cordaites

Conifers

Ginkgo

Glossopteris

Cycadeoids

PSILOPHYTES
Zosterophyllum

PSILOPHYTES
Rhynia

Blue green bacteria

Bacteria**

CHLOROPHYTA
Green algae

*at least 1 billion years ago
**3½ billion years ago

Era	Period
Cenozoic	Holocene 0.01
	1.8 Pleisto
	Pliocene Miocene Oligocer Eocene Paleocen 65
Precambrian	Cretace 140
	Jurassic 195
	Triassic 245
	Permian 280
	Carboni 345
Mesozoic	Devonia 410
	Silurian 440
	Ordovic 500
	Cambri 570
Paleozoic	Precamb 700***

EVOLUTION OF THE PROTIST AND ANIMAL KINGDOMS

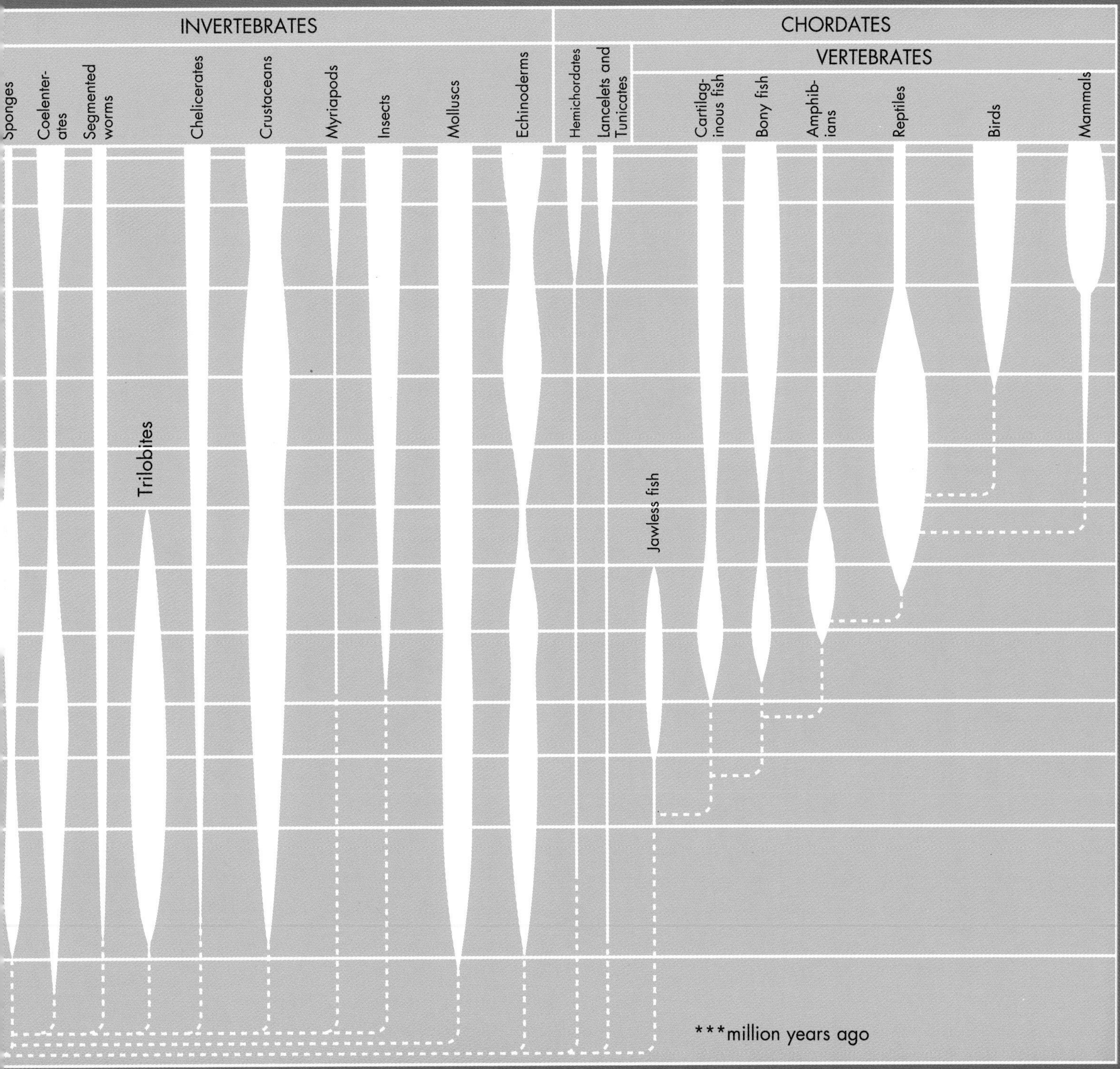

INVERTEBRATES

CHORDATES

VERTEBRATES

Sponges

Coelenterates

Segmented worms

Chelicerates

Crustaceans

Myriapods

Insects

Molluscs

Echinoderms

Hemichordates

Lancelets and Tunicates

Cartilaginous fish

Bony fish

Amphibians

Reptiles

Birds

Mammals

Trilobites

Jawless fish

***million years ago